From the #1 Motivated Author

THE ART OF
GETTING PAID
As Often As Possible

I0402579

5 Simple Steps To Putting
You On The Financial Map

Dr. Titus C. Wright

"But you shall remember the Lord your God: for it is he that gives you the power to get wealth..."
-Deuteronomy 8:18

CONTENTS

Introduction   9

A Thought   12

Inspired words   17

Chapter One   19 Five Steps To Prosperity In Life
Step 1   20 Ask Yourself Why

Step 2   25 The Answer Is You

Step 3   29 Turn Should Into Must

Step 4   30 Be The Change

Step 5   35 Be Contribution Minded
Chapter Two   41 The Conclusion

About The Author 43

Other Books by Dr. Titus C. Wright 45

INTRODUCTION

How many times would you like to get paid in a week, month or year? I hope you said as often as possible. The art of getting paid avails itself to much thinking, focused work and lots of creativity. We are not talking about any regular pay check here. I'm talking about money that an average job really can't afford to pay you. If you really want to get paid then its real work that you have to do. This is why you should go to work after coming home from your job. Your Job and Your Work are usually two different things.

Your job and your work could be separate. (usually your current job is not your *True Work* (unless you are a doctor, lawyer or something you purposely took years in school to learn.) Do you know the work you are called to do in your life? What is your true work? It is usually aligned with your gift. Do you know your gifts? (There are more than one. Sometimes a Campaign of gifts are in you in the same area). These seem like an awful lot of questions that need to be an swered. I assure you we will be answering all of these concerns in the upcoming paragraphs. Your gifts protect you.

I Timothy 4:14 "Neglect not the gift that is in thee, which was given thee by prophecy, with the laying on of the hands of the presbytery"

Find your gift (True Work) and add to it. You can add knowledge, skill, professionalism, character and ethics. Always put your gift in front of your education and drive it for ward. (Use education as the fuel, to propel your gift). Most successful people are operating within their gifts. (Bill Gates, Warren Buffet, Tiger Woods, Michael Jordan, Oprah Winfrey, Serena Williams, Steve Harvey etc.). Learn to Operate within your gift. Whatever you do best naturally is a gift. This is how you perfect the Art of Getting Paid as Often as Possible.

You cannot be fired from Your Work like you can from your Job. Your job is what you do, but your gift is who your really are. Finding your gift. (What can you do that comes easy and maybe harder for everyone else.) Discovering what makes you special is in finding what you can do with very little effort. (When you can do something a little bit better than everybody else, then you have found one of your gifts)

Develop the gift that you have passion for. You may not have passion for all of your gifts. Develop the gift you really want to work with. Something you'd do for hours on end without thinking of time and effort. Don't confuse your job with your gift. People don't necessarily want you per se, they want your Gift. (Don't take it personally). You come with the gift. Some men get destroyed when they lose their job not knowing their true work resides within them. Your gift will make you a success if developed. Stop trying to become a success and start trying to become *Valuable*.

Money is attracted to Value. Become a person of *value*. The more valuable you are the more successful you will become. Increase your knowledge of something you really like to do that people really want. Specialize and focus. Become Significant, original and unique in your Gift/work. Your gift will take you places where you really couldn't go on your own. Your gift will make you successful if you use it well. Operate within your gift!

"A mans gift makes room for him, and brings him before great men" -Proverbs 18:16

Don't quit your current job when you come up with a bright idea. Here is another passage from my favorite book.

Ecclesiastes 11:6 " In the morning sew thy seed, and in the evening withhold not thine hand: for thou knoweth not whether shall prosper, either this or that, or whether they both shall be alike good"

Keep your job until you can perfect your gift, that it can sustain you. Have faith to yourself, don't drag people down with reckless faith. Do not leave your job until you are secure in your work. *Be smart!*

Are you going to work tomorrow or are you going to a job? Your job tells you how much you should make. Your gift and true work tells you to make as much as you want. If you really want to know the *Art of Getting Paid*, find your gift. Whatever you were created to become is not outside of you but on the inside of you.

"Your future is not around or even ahead of you, but it is in you. When a person finds their true gift, they can make it anywhere.

You don't go to work, you go to a job. Your true work travels with you. The opportunity to get paid well will always be within you. An auto mechanic doesn't need to be in any one particular city to perform his work. If he is really good at what he does, he will always have work. The more *value* you give yourself, the more the world will pay for it. Increase your knowledge in what you do and become more valuable.

Remember to focus on what you are good at, don't be a generalist. Find your greatness by trying different things then stick to what you do the very best. Don't follow your passion, follow your gift and make it your passion.

"Dreams are free, Sweat equity sold separately"
-Steve Harvey

A THOUGHT:

By following these simple steps, you can reach a higher level of success. Prosperity is just around the corner. Ultimately, it's up to you to allow this information to change your circumstances. After years of reading and studying hundreds of books by some of the most successful financial gurus, I realize that they all basically give much of the same advice. Success does leave clues. Their obvious overwhelming success is the proof that it works. I will be quoting lots of these people but chances are, they weren't the first to have said it.

Starting your own business isn't an exact science. It is more of an art. Successful entrepreneurs are a very diverse group of people. You should seriously consider either becoming an entrepreneur or investor. In the long run, it would be to your best financial advantage. You can have the opportunity to be self empowered.

With all of this being said, you've got to be cautious when being approached about a so-called business opportunity. You need to be prepared to do your homework or *"Due Diligence."* Regardless of how good a business opportunity sounds, remember that no one really cares about your financial situation more than you do. Your success or failure depends upon the decisions you make for yourself. Take responsibility for your own financial acumen. *"Success is a journey, not a destination"-Unknown*

It is true that nobody is going to come to your rescue when you are broke, busted, and disgusted. However, I dobelieve there are plenty of opportunities out there that will fit into your plan, if you have one. The key word here is *plan*. You've got to have a plan or strategy to get where you want to be. Author Wallace D. Wattles mentions in his many books that getting rich is the result of "*doing things in a certain way*." You have got to associate yourself with either a product, service, or concept. If you look around you will notice that everybody is selling something. There are only two transactions taking place in the world 24 hours a day. Either you are buying or selling something. If you are employed, then you are selling your time for dollars. If you are a teacher (as in my case a professor), then you are selling your knowledge. What are your abilities, skills, or talents? What do you plan to sell or have to offer?

They often say you have to have a better idea to succeed. This is not always true. You can find something that is already doing well and do that. An I-Phone isn't the invention of the telephone. As Alexander Graham Bell already did that. The I-phone represents an incremental change from past technologies. This includes the internet, TV, camera, video, game arcade and so much more. You don't always have to reinvent the wheel. There are tons of examples of people doing what you already want to do. There are biographies you can read, people you can see or hear about that are involved in doing the same thing you desire to do. I say watch and study them. Study the way these people think and conduct themselves. Notice how hard they work to achieve the results that they get. Never underestimate how much massive action is necessary to achieve your dream.

Don't be a "lone ranger". Don't try and do it all by yourself. Others will be compelled by your leadership to join you. Once you set up your structure and take action towards your vision, people will want to help. Communicate your vision clearly to make sure it is understood. Finding the best people for your wealth team is crucial for your success. I believe people who try to become *"self made"* always fail because they are missing a key ingredient, *"people"*. As they say, "The speed of the leader is the speed of the team". Be a team player by joining others in their wealth pursuits as well. You will come to understand that helping others helps *you*. Everything does come back, so take charge and lead your wealth. Focus your energies into productive tasks, not on unproductive busy activities.

As you read this book, I want you to realize that you need others to help you along your success journey. Don't focus on money but focus on quality service, and added value. Money will come as a result of what you bring to the market place. Ninety percent of all success comes from having a great attitude. Be willing to work smart and hard. You have to get off your butt and start moving toward your goal now! When you know where you're going and what you want, the universe has a tendency to get out of your way.

You need to make up your mind that being successful is a must and you have got to *do* it. Begin using words such as, *I Can, It is Possible, It's Not too Hard or Difficult for Me!* Let's be totally honest with ourselves by forgetting our ego, eliminating our pride, and being willing to get down to business *right now*. Let's try our best to focus on creating a product or service of value first and then offering it to others. Condition yourself for success. Experience a paradigm shift in habits.

What is wealth to you? You need to specifically define what wealth means to you and create an achievable plan. How much money would it take for you to feel financially independent and successful? Success has to be planned and earned. The secret to this whole thing in a nutshell is, if you focus on success, wealth will always show up. If a professional boxer keeps knocking out his opponents, wealth will always follow him. This does not happen the other way around. Success is the generator of wealth. If you keep winning, you keep getting paid. The more success, the more pay. This also happens at work too.

Sometimes you have to qualify yourself for a raise by first doing more consistently, then you can ask for a raise later. If you keep this in mind you will always be prosperous. Don't get the order mixed up. No unsuccessful person has ever become wealthy. I really want you to become wealthy so badly! Whether you know it or not, people are depending on you to become rich. This is because many of them don't have the faith and motivation that you have. They see something in you and need that something to inspire them to get moving. Success is a great motivator. Success speaks louder than words.

In order to live your dreams, as Les Brown often says, you've got to first build one. If you build your dream effectively, you can then live in it.

"Build your dream so you can live your dream"
-Steve Harvey *(Steve Harvey show 2017)*.

You have the faith to start getting paid big or you would not be reading this book. Open your eyes, see right in front of you. Look for those magic moments. You will affect people around you because you are about to develop and enhance your extraordinary psychology to succeed. Start seeing great opportunities otherwise disguised as problems or challenges. You've got to prepare for where you want to go.

"When you change the way you look at things, the way you look at things change" - Dr. Wayne Dyer.

Pay attention to these upcoming 5 steps. They will help guide you toward ultimate success and the true *Art of Getting Paid as Often as Possible!* Now, let's get busy!

*"Do what you can as well as you can do it,
even if it is something you don't like"*
-Bob Proctor

"The easier I am on myself, the harder life is on me."
-Steve Chandler

*"Some say, if I had more money I would have
a better plan, but it should be, If I had a better plan,
I would have more money"*
-Brian Tracy

"If your ship doesn't come in, Swim out to meet it"
-Les Brown

"How you do anything, is how you do everything"
-Jack Canfield

*"When it comes to infinity, you can never
take more than your share"*
-Bob Proctor

*"Imagination and knowledge is the key
to becoming successful"*
-Donald J. Trump

NOTES

Chapter One

5 STEPS TO TRUE PROSPERITY IN LIFE

"The only way to become wealthy is to add more value in other peoples lives than anyone else is adding."

-Tony Robbins

T he **Art Of Getting Paid As Often As Possible** can now be turned into a must statement. This gives you all the reasons and certain ways to become very successful. If you want to make any kind of impact on others in the world, then you need to become a wealthy person. When Indian guru Swami Satchidananda arrived in America in 1969 and landed at the New York airport, he looked around and said, *"They live in paradise, yet they'll never know it."*

Sometimes it is difficult to see the abundance in front of you because of familiarity. As they say, "You can't see the forest for the trees". You are the only one who is responsible for moving your life forward. Open your eyes and begin to change the pattern of what you focus on daily. That's the secret. You can actually generate abundance in your life by having an abundance mentality. Changing your thought patterns is important in order to prosper. Abundant ideas come from abundant thought patterns, not from scarcity thought patterns. Are you aware that poverty breeds on poverty, and abundance breeds more abundance? As Bob Proctor would say, *"You need to experience a paradigm shift"*. There is an old saying that states, "The rich get richer and the poor get poorer." However, this is a true statement and the bible confirms it. *"For whoever has, to him more will be given, but whoever does not have, even what he has will be taken away from him"* [1] - (Mark 4:25).

Step 1: *Ask Yourself, WHY? (What is Your Why?)*

You need to start with *Why?* not *How?* or *What?* at first. Ask yourself, "Why do I want to be Successful?" The question *Why?* gives you your higher purpose and clarifies the vision you have for yourself. I asked that same question years ago and it helped me to refocus on my strategic mission. The answer to *Why?* comes from the heart. The question *How?* is the action to accomplish your Why? The question *What?* is the result of it all. All three are important but *Why?* is your inspiration which is the fuel that gets the engine moving.

Service to others should be your main priority when starting a business. If you go into a profession with service in mind, financial abundance won't be far behind. This unselfish thinking generates all kinds of wonderful ideas that will just pop into your head. This has happened to me so many times. Never be motivated by money when thinking of new ideas. Let service to others be your motivation.

I believe Bill Gates, Microsoft founder, did not start out trying to be the second richest man on the planet. Thanks to Jeff Bezos being the richest (Amazon founder). It was one of those things that just happened because of all the service he was providing. He just wanted to write software for small personal computers, which has helped hundreds of millions all over the world. Facebook founder, Mark Zuckenberg, had no idea the social website created in his college dorm would eventually be worth over 500 billion dollars today. Money was not his motivator. Facebook is free to all worldwide. Advertisers noticed the traffic generated and made him a multi billionaire many times over.

"Anyone with sight can count the seeds of an apple, but a person with true vision can count the apples in a seed" Les Brown.

Why, changes everything as it has changed the entire Amerrican legal system in the mid 1800's. Dr. Isaac Ray asked that *Why?* question and became the father of *Forensic Psychiatry.* Thus, the legal term *MENS REA* was born. *Mens Rea* means *intent or guilty mind.* Dr. Ray asked, *"Why are these people committing such unheard of crimes?"* Prior to this question, *What?* and *How?* were the only considerations. They were asking *What was done? and How was it accomplished? case closed!* They were putting mentally ill criminals to death! and giving others long prison terms. The *Mens Rea* term asks questions such as, '*Was the crime premeditated? Was mental illness an involved factor? Did the defendant know what he or she was actually doing?'*

After the *Mens Rea* term was introduced, the insanity defense became a huge factor. Tons of tests associated with the insanity defense have been created as well. The question *Why?* is now a consideration in most criminal cases. The *Mens Rea* term has been added as the second of three major requirements in a criminal *Prima Facie* case. *Mens Rea* is one of the elements now included to justify submission of guilt of a defendant to a jury. There has been a plethora of defenses using the required mens rea term to either down grade serious offenses or release defendants to psychiatric facilities. The only term that negates the *Mens Rea* requirement are crimes where strict liability is imposed. Dr Isaac Ray dared to ask *WHY!*

What is your Why? What is your reasoning for doing what you do in business? Can you communicate this in your promotions, adverting or Public relations? Inspiration from Why? lasts longer than motivation of What? Asking Why? is important.

I am writing this portion of the book on what happens to be Dr. Martin Luther King Jr's birthday (January 18th). It brings back the *I Have a Dream Speech* at the Lincoln Memorial every time. During that time, people were motivated by his vision of hope and inspiration. Hundreds of thousands of people showed up to hear his speech. They were inspired by his dream of freedom and equality.

Suppose, Dr. King had tried to motivate them with an, "I have a twelve step plan!" speech, they would have stayed home. Your *Why?* infuses people if it is strong enough. You don't want a weak *Why?* Your *Why?* has to be inclusive and unselfish. It has to point to a higher purpose of meaning that includes others. Have a distinct clarity of *Why?* Your *Why?* is a belief, then your *How?* comes into play to get it done. Your *Why?* is your invisible force, passion and high energy.

It's not always *What?* you do, but *Why?* you do it that needs to be communicated in order to get help from others. If I needed help moving a big rock down a steep hill and asked people for assistance, many of them would have excuses for not helping. If I told them *Why?* I needed their help such as, it will block the river from flooding and destroying all of our homes. This gives them an invested interest in the project. They would not only help but encourage others to get involved as well. This is what you have to do when it comes to your business. You should run your business based on the Why? factor. Give people a reason to buy from you. Get people to understand why they need your product or service. Inspiration isn't something you have but it's something you generate. Your product or service needs to be the object of generated inspiration. You must give your business a meaning and a real purpose for being or existing.

Sam Walton, founder of Wal-Mart Corporation, started his first store in Harrison Arkansas, I believe he wasn't focused on having one of the most successful businesses in the world. Sam Walton focused on service and trying to be the leader in giving people the lowest prices possible for quality merchandise. He had a low-cost merchandise strategy. Again, I would recommend that you start with a service business. You may be asking me, *Why?* would I say that? A service business usually has less overhead. A product business involves a lot of processes as well as paying for and maintaining inventory. Suppose the inventory does not sell? You will be stuck with a lot of useless merchandise. If you create a service business first, you could decrease your expenses. Once you start making money, you can always go into a product business later. Only invest in a product business when you have funds.

Your mission is to get people to understand why people need your service if it is good. Try to give people what they want and help them get what they need. Create a service with a good enough *Why?* that will give customers something to believe in. Your income is in direct proportion to the service you provide. Doing your best puts you on the next level. Set the target, reach it first then move it up a notch. A leader must clearly communicate why the company or business exists in terms beyond it's product or service.

Steve Jobs, Apple founder, was a real *WHY?* man. His signature trait was always in promoting the image of the product as opposed to the actual product. He created a culture centered around his passion for great products. He was on a mission and had a real purpose. We knew what he was about. He was about creating products that he would want to use himself. This sparked his passion with huge profits waiting in the wings.

The Harley Davidson company has also created a culture around it's products. People get tattoos on their bodies of the Harley Davidson logo and they don't even own a bike. They understand the reason behind the logo. It represents something of which they can relate to. It represents freedom and the boldness to be who you are. Dare to be different as an individual. This is their message. Some people want to be part of a group with a culture that represents an image of a world class leader since 1903. The company represents an overall experience, not just a good product. The Harley Davidson company promotes great business ethics. The company has an amazing *Why?* for the reason they are in business. They have a true purpose that goes beyond selling the best quality motorcycles in the world. The company believes in customer satisfaction, and going beyond expectations of all buyers. Keeping their promises, being fair, and being quality driven is all part of their mission and vision statement. What is your *WHY?* for wanting to be in business for yourself?

Until the question *Why?* is passionately answered, there will always be lots of questions left on the table. Always ask "Why? should people buy from me?" Would you buy from you? Know this: People want to share your values and beliefs, not just the quality of your service or product. What is your cause? Try and find out what people really want and give it to them. In return people will help you to get what you want: *success and prosperity.*

Step #2: *The Answer Is YOU!*

At age 25, Jim Rohn was asked by his mentor why he wasn't doing well financially. He responded by showing him his paycheck stating, *"This is all they pay"*. His mentor replied that his statement was not exactly correct. Jim's rebuttal was, *"No, this is all they pay. You can't do well with a paycheck like that!"* His mentor looked at him again and said, *"That's not all they pay, that's all they pay you!"* He let him know that some people at his job make five times that amount. He goes on to tell him that if he were to add more value to himself, it would increase his paycheck and make a significant difference in his life. *"To have more, become more."*-Jim Rohn.

If you were to change yourself you would be able to change your entire circumstance. The operative words here are *You* and *Change*. It's not the economy, it's not taxes, the industry, high prices, interest rates, or any other external factors. It's *You!* Stop making excuses and stop blaming everybody else and take full responsibility for yourself. Let's work on *You*. This is the source of the entire problem. If you would change your thinking you can change your life. If you have a job, don't dress for the job you have. Dress for the job you want. If you are not doing well in life then you have got to be willing to make massive changes in your psychology (which affects your physiology). This internal change will change everything for you. As I said earlier in this chapter, having a scarcity mentality creates more scarcity in your life. A scarcity mentality shapes your physical appearance. You will physically look broke in your disposition. People can see you coming a mile away. Your mental state has the power to shape you mentally and physically. As psychologists tell us, "Ninety percent of our communication is non verbal." When people look at you, what do they see? If poverty can be seen from a distance, so can having an Abundance Mindset. As Michael Jackson sung, *"Make that change. I'm talking about the man in the mirror."*

NOTES

"Don't focus on what needs to be done, focus on the person you need to become to get it done" -Jim Rohn

Another thing to consider is *that* you have got to stop asking lousy questions of yourself. Questions such as, *"Why am I so poor, broke or a loser?"* The answer would come back as, *"because you're an idiot!" This* is not conducive to your self improvement. Theses answers won't really help you. You need to start creating a positive wealth feeling and consciousness within yourself. Ask positive questions and you'll get positive answers. Try and see yourself differently in your own mind. It won't cost you a dime to think positively and create a feeling of abundance.

If a good idea is going to pop into your mind, it will develop within an abundance mindset and not in scarcity mode. Success can happen at any moment within this abundant state. I literally went from the brink of financial disaster to earning thousands of dollars in a matter of a few hours. I remember over ten years ago when I was having serious challenges in my business. I went to a restaurant just to think. I grabbed a napkin and started jotting down notes. An hour later, when I came out of that restaurant, I was so pumped up and excited with vision and hope, I thought I was going to explode. I went back to my office and was infused with a brand new strategy. My staff got excited and we all started making money immediately. I was given a new internal infusion. I then knew exactly why I had been failing. I then knew how to rekindle success again.

You need to do a SWOT Analysis on yourself. This analysis looks at he Strengths, Weaknesses, Opportunities available to you now and possible Threats you can recognize. Make a detailed record on a piece of paper of all of your strengths. This includes all of your assets (drivers license, degrees, skills, God given gifts and talents, etc.). Secondly, list your weaknesses. This is not to put yourself down but to help you see yourself more clearly. Admit your weaknesses to yourself. Know exactly what you are good at and what you really are bad at. Get someone to help you get to where you want to go. Find people who are good at the things that you are not good at. This helps you to keep going while eliminating road blocks. So many people stop at their own limitations. Be wise enough to ask for help. This allows you to keep moving forward as you focus on your strengths. Be insightful and honest enough to know when you need assistance from others. Warren Buffet says he's smart in spots, so he stays around those spots. Having insight is serious business. Insight represents understanding. The Bible says that, "...*In all of your getting, get understanding.*"₂ Know your weaknesses!

Thirdly, list your opportunities. You need to always be on the lookout for opportunities everywhere you go. There are opportunities everywhere. Lastly, be honest in listing your threats. This includes people and areas that are doing you no good. You know who and where they are. You want to maximize your opportunities and minimize your threats. Change yourself incrementally. This means that your change needs to happen gradually. It's not done overnight. You can multiply your income by creating more value in yourself toward the market place. Invest in yourself to make yourself more valuable. Start helping someone do something today. It could be anything. You need to start moving. Once you get some kind of momentum, other ideas will pop into your head. Remember, one good idea can make you millions. Read, study, change your attitude and never stop learning. Learn to work harder on yourself than you do on your job.

Step #3: *Turn Your SHOULD, Into MUST*

The wealthy people that I know are relatively quiet. They are always working on a new idea or involved in some kind of investment. A person would have to pry the information out of them to get them to talk about it. Most wealthy people are quick to hear and slow to speak. They already know what they know, their busy trying to find out what others know. So they listen. Everything they do seems urgent. I used to think, "Hey, what's the rush or urgency! You're already rich." This is probably why they are so rich! They always strike while the iron is hot. As Teddy Roosevelt would say, *"Walk softly and carry a big stick."*

You need to start imagining the possibilities of becoming successful. You may be saying to yourself, "I know, I know, I should own a house. I should go back to school and get my degree. I should be saving money and investing, etc." If this is you, then you need to turn those *Shoulds* into *Musts*. As long as it is something that you think you should do, then it probably won't get done. You have to make it a *Must*. Make your dreams, goals and aspirations something you must get done. When I was in college and graduate school, I made it a *Must* to never miss a class and only get an A in every course. I was on the Dean's List the entire time. I did this for nearly eight consecutive years. I never even considered anything less than excellence of myself. The word *Must* ignites **action.**

You only get what you must have and not a penny more! This entire process starts with one thing, *You*! Make it a *Must* in deciding what you are going to do and how it's going to be. The word *Should* is weak! It is only a suggestion. You need to turn that suggestion into a reality. You *Must* achieve, succeed and become prosperous. This has to be intrinsic before it can be manifested physically in your life. A sky-scraper building can only be built when it is finished. Before a physical building is constructed, the plans and the architectural rendering of the structure, design and layout has to be finished first. This also works for the physical manifestation of your success. You *Must* first achieve it intrinsically. You *Must* see it as a reality in your own mind first!

Step #4: *BE The Change.*

I'm sure by now you have heard this saying at least a million times. The entire statement reads, *"Be the change you wish to see in the world"* *-Gandhi.* As we already mentioned, you are the only one responsible for your life and the decisions that you make. People do have fears and doubts in themselves about the idea of becoming more than what they are. *"As human beings, our greatness lies not so much in being able to remake the world – that is the myth of the atomic age – as in being able to remake ourselves."* -Gandhi

It is difficult to take massive action towards a dream when there is no confidence. It's like running through the forest with all of your might having your eyes closed. Eventually you're going to run into a tree or worse. You would be cautious at every move. *"Confidence is the ability along with the attitude and willingness to perform"* -Dee-Pak Chopra

Being grateful is the key to lasting *Wealth.* Feed on deep and profound gratitude. The more you give thanks the more good things will come to you by showing gratitude. The mental attitude of gratitude draws the mind into closeness with the source from which the blessing comes. The law of gratitude is in line with the law of action and reaction. To create measureless substance one needs to show measureless gratitude. You cannot exercise much power without gratitude. Showing gratitude does not look to take credit. Make showing gratitude a habit for everything that comes to you. The closer we are to the source of wealth (God), the more wealth will be manifested toward us.

"In order to move to the next level, you must show gratitude for where you are now." -Steve Harvey (TBN, Harvey)

Money can come and go, but who you have become in creating wealth lasts forever. I often recreate (*fake*) popular magazine covers with my photo on the front. Covers such as, Forbes, Entrepreneur, Inc. Money and so many other publications. I use these as dream boards. They are very motivating for me. Of course, it's not about the money, as Donald Trump often says, *"It's just a way of keeping score."* He recounts that he doesn't do things just for the money but enjoys what he does and has a real passion for it. He says he makes more money than he would have made if he was just after the money. Be a real leader with a vision that can be communicated to others. A real leader does not have to compete with anyone else but himself/herself. Constantly try to be better than you were yesterday and better tomorrow than you were today. When you compete against yourself, then people will help you. When you compete against others, no one will want to help you because you've made them your competition. Be a creator and/or a trail blazer. No one is just going to give you what you want on a silver platter. As a great civil rights leader, Mahatma Gandhi said, *"You need to be the change you want to take place in your own life."*

NOTES

Step #5: *Be Contribution Minded*

Everybody wants to be rich but will it really make you happy? Even if money doesn't really make you happy, everyone wants to find out for themselves. Early last year, there was a $1.6 billion jackpot up for grabs, the biggest lottery amount in history. Three groups eventually won. Wow, unheard of! Whoever won it, needs to hurry up and try and become successful or they won't get to keep it. Did you know that ninety percent of lottery winners go broke within five years time? Why does this happen? They have not learned to become successful and wealthy. They may still have a poverty consciousness. Riches are external but wealth is internal and is more sustaining. You've heard the analogy, "If I give a person a fish, they eat for a day. However, if you teach a person how to fish, they eat for a life time." This knowledge is called wealth.

People think they need more money to solve their money problems. *NEWS FLASH -Money Does Not Solve Money Problems. Your Mind Solves Money Problems.* Never use the same thing that initially got you in that bad financial situation to get you out of it. So money does not solve money problems, *You* do! Get wisdom and change your mindset in handling money. As you change your negative attitude about money,   you will begin to feel more financially comfortable. Becoming rich and staying rich takes work. As a matter of fact, through my experience, I've found it was easier to make money and harder to keep it. My once epicurean spending habits hurt me.

The reason why you may not have extra money in your pocket is that you may not be accustomed to having it around keeping you company. It is burning a hole in your pocket. Some people will spend every penny that they have and once it's all gone, they then feel at ease. Many people feel it's hard to relax with a pocket full of money. As long as that money is unspent, they are on edge. Believe me, I know about this because I was one of those people. You can overcome these bad habits because it is part of the process, in order for you to actually become rich. Wealthy habits can be developed. Admit and fix your weaknesses. Don't be afraid of the truth!

If you can think successful thoughts, then you can become a successful person. If you can imagine yourself doing something, then you can actually *do* it. If you cannot imagine it, then don't expect for it to happen. All of the wealth in the world is spent on feeling "good". When some people become bored or want to feel good, they go shopping. People buy new cars or other toys they think they need just to get that good initial feeling. Admittedly, buying new stuff does give you a real "high" but it doesn't last. This does allow a person temporary fulfillment and brief satisfaction until the newness quickly wears off. I suggest you cut out the middle man, save your money and just start feeling good for free. Start feeling like a success now!

I remember wanting to be on television. I began imagining myself actually having a T.V. show. I had to see it and of course *believe* it too. As a result, it became a reality. I believe visualizing it caused me to move toward that direction. Do you know what you want or where you are going? You just have to imagine yourself *being* there. Try to visualize it. This cannot be just a vague thought. Take time, sit down and daydream about what you want. Then try to see it happening. As it was said earlier, in order to be a winner, you'll have to think like a winner.

Don't be afraid to imagine yourself being successful. It won't cost you a cent. Go ahead, put up those dream boards. See yourself becoming successful and wealthy. Get an image ofsomething in your mind, use pictures you cut out of magazines, travel brochures or from the internet. And dream, dream, dream. Try and dream **big and then start small**.

Of course there is nothing wrong with feeling good. However, you should only buy things when you already feel good, not to **make** you feel good. Life is short and "quality" of life is just as important as "quantity" of life. Who wants to live to be a hundred years old struggling financially and constantly worrying about paying bills? This would be a miserable existence. I simply call that *torture.*

Elevate your thoughts and opportunities will follow. The Bible states that, *"As a man thinks in his heart, so is he."*[2] Your mind leads your body. Before you can do anything it has to first become a thought. You must begin to speak positively and start feeling like you are already successful. In 2018 when Barack Obama won the election, he was sworn in because he was the president. He had already won and was given the oath of the office. While he was running for the office, he'd already claimed the presidency in his campaign speeches. He kept saying, *"My White House".*

When you hear on the news of a sensational discovery or innovative product, this didn't happen overnight. It may have been publicized overnight, but it may have taken years of research and study to create the result. Some newly discovered singers call themselves, a ten year overnight sensation. A child prodigy didn't graduate from college at age 15 to become smart, He graduated at age 15 because he was already smart. Let your success first start in your mind. You succeed because you are already a success. Success is created as a result of a plan in place. Being *"Lucky"* can be defined as when opportunity meets preparation. This is what they said about Bruce Lee, *"He was always preparing for a fight that will never happen."* He became a superstar. Be prepared to do that which is necessary to become what you want. If it's more skills, education, confidence, drive or whatever, Go Get It! Your life will change when you change!

NOTES

"It's never too late to be what you might have been"
-George Eliot

Chapter Two

CONCLUSION:

"If you don't pay the price for success you'll pay the price for failure".

- Zig Ziglar

Congratulations! By now, you should be seeing changes in your life. Some people believe that the amount of money a person makes is important. I believe what you do with whatever money you have is more important. However, doing what you really love while meeting a need and serving others is the *Key* to fulfillment. This is extremely important! These practical steps are just the beginning.

This book's subtitle does mention *Wealth, Success,* and *Prosperity.* These three appear to be the same, however, they are not. Wealth is moving forward with no particular state of emotion. It could be summed up as cash flow. Success is an internal feeling or state of being. It is a state of mind derived from fulfillment. Prosperity is the combination of them both being in balance and congruent with each other. It is possible to be wealthy without feeling successful. Success gives wealth meaning. Inherited wealth needs meaning attached to it. This is why so many wealthy people become philanthropists, give to charities or start foundations. Now that you have completed this reading, use the information in this book as a reference. Refer to it often. Keep it close to you for continued guidance in making wise decisions towards the *Art of Getting Paid As Often As Possible.*
Congratulations and continued SUCCESS!

ABOUT THE AUTHOR

Dr. Titus C. Wright is a motivational speaker, expert sales trainer, university professor, and CEO of Wright Media Group. He is the inspired author of *How To Get The Man/Woman of Your Dreams, Waiting To Be Great, Forced To Be Rich* and *Why You Should Be Rich.* Titus motivates thousands of people per week with his *Positive Force* Youtube videos. magazine publications, and self help books. He is blessed to have earned two Masters degrees in business administration/management. He also received a (Ph.D.) in Christian Education. Titus has dedicated his life to personal self development and in helping others find their true purpose and passion. He has appeared on local and national television shows, numerous radio programs and in newsprint/magazines. He lives in Pennsylvania with his lovely wife, Coral.

THE ART OF GETTING PAID is Titus's sixth nationwide book release. This book is considered, one of the most revealing, straight forward and helpful to date. It is said by many that his books are worth their weight in *Pure Gold*. His multi-media organization continues to thrive due to these God-given rules. He adheres to his own advice and has been able to implement these concepts in his own life and business. Titus believes that, prosperity isn't about owning things. It's about nothing owning you! Contact email: twrightmediagroup@gmail.com
Available for corporate and academic speaking engagements.

Other Books By Dr. Titus C. Wright

Business Success

ALL NEW! TITLES!

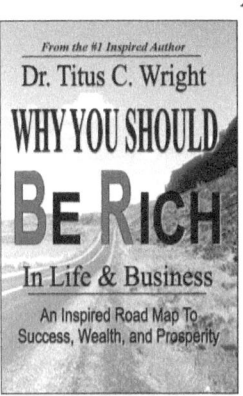

Relationship Success

How To Get The Woman Of Your Dreams
& Man of Your Dreams

Two, One of a Kind Books That Every Person Should Have In Their Personal Collection